GULLY
Celebrity Chef

By Jon Cleave

Published in 2006
© 2006 Jonathan Cleave

www.thegullery.co.uk

All rights reserved. No part of this publication may be reproduced
or transmitted in any form or by any means, electronic or mechanical, including
photocopy, recording or any information storage and retrieval system,
without prior permission in writing from the publisher.

ISBN-10: 0-9553165-3-7
ISBN-13: 978-0-9553165-3-1

Text and illustrations copyright © 2006 Jonathan Cleave
The rights of Jonathan Cleave to be identified as author and illustrator of this work has been
asserted by him in accordance with the Copyright, Designs and Patents Act 1988.
Design by Brad Waters www.bradwaters.com
Printed in the Westcountry by The Printing Press

For Libby

Do you like the telly? So do I, and so does the princess. We love it, and spend loads of evenings up in the gullery, peeping in through the window at Mrs Baker's.

We call it the gullivision!

But you know, you must be careful how much gullivision you watch, because it can be really dangerous. Those soap operas can send you completely barking mad, and if you sit still in the armchair for too long, your toes will drop off one by one, and if you have the volume too loud your ears will shrivel up like little prawns, or if you sit too close you could catch a terrible disease like tellysquint or screen scurvy. And if you don't believe me just because I'm only a gull, go ask your mums and dads if it ain't true…

Gully and the Princess watching one of their favourite programmes

So the princess and I don't watch the gullivision *too* much, but we do have our favourites. And of course that's another thing that could make you very poorly, watching the wrong sort of programmes, the sort that are not fresh, wholesome and organic, and full of vitamins and protein and fibre and all that stuff, so we are very careful only to watch the healthiest options available.

Like cookery programmes.

Just the other week, Mrs Baker left our cottage to head off to town on the bus, and as always she kindly put out a snack for me. A nice, big, fat, icky, sticky, treacly, treacle tart actually, like we'd seen them making on the gullivision the night before.

On a doily, on a dish.

On her windowsill.

By her window.

Which was left open….

All right, all right, I know what you're thinking, but no I did not *immediately* hop in through the open window and create utter havoc in Mrs Baker's front room.

No, first it was my duty to eat the tart.

I started with a little peck. It was not the best thing I have ever tasted. To be honest, I found it to be rather sweet and sickly and gooey, and not at all to my taste. It was quite a disappointment really.

Anyway, I whoomphed the lot down in one gigantic gulp, just to get it over and done with, even the paper doily which took some swallowing I can tell you but, hey, you know what I'm going to say…

I did it because I'm a gull, right, and it would have been rude not to!

Then, what a treat, I saw what looked like a nice chunky bar of chocolate just inside the window.

Mrs Baker's nice front room

Well, when I say just inside the window, that's not strictly true. It was on the other side of the room, on the sideboard on top of the gullivision.

The thing is, I know she would have wanted me to eat that as well as the treacle tart.

I took a look up, then down, the street, and seeing there was no one about I hopped in off the windowsill, through the window and onto the back of a nice soft chair.

I looked around inquisitively. It was a bit dark in there, but nice. Comfy really, a bit like the gullery, although maybe she could have done with a few more sticks and twigs and bits of stinky dried seaweed and faded crisp bags and old rope straggles strewn around, just to give it that extra homely feel. Thinking about it, I *did* have some spare back up in the gullery…

Oh don't worry. I didn't do it. Look, I like Mrs Baker, ok? Besides, I never had the time anyway.

I hopped across the floor and flapped up onto the sideboard and picked up the bar of chocolate with my beak.

It was a bit hard!

I picked up the bar of chocolate

I couldn't manage to break off any of the chunks, so I lifted it up and then dropped it, in the hope that a piece might just snap off.

What happened next gave me a bit of a shock.

The chocolate bar hit the floor…clunk! and the gullivision on the sideboard next to me flickered into life. It was like magic!

I settled down to watch the programme.

Now don't get me wrong, I'm sure they are very nice, but if you were allowed to make a TV programme about anything, would you make one about a stick insect? I mean, they don't move about much, do they? Wouldn't it be better to make a programme about us gulls? We're exciting, fun, a little mischievous maybe, certainly clever (do you know of another bird who tells silly stories?) and, if I may say so, rather handsome.

Anyway, I watched the programme for thirty seconds. During this time the stick insect didn't do anything at all, not even something an ordinary stick could do. It didn't fall out of a tree. It didn't get snapped in half. It didn't get rubbed against another stick by a boy scout to start a fire. I began to feel bored. I decided that it was time for a change and dropped the bar of chocolate again. The magic worked once more.

This time there was a smart looking lady on the gullivision, and I can't read all that well but I'm sure at the bottom of the screen it said 'News', whatever that is. I kept watching.

'And now,' she said, 'over to Dartmouth where they have been experiencing a major airborne problem.'

A major airborne problem

'Yes,' said a man. 'Thank you Nina. The resident seagull population here is about to outnumber the resident human population, and that is causing big problems. What happened to you sir?'

'I just been up on our roof to try and get rid of 'em,' said a man who appeared to be totally covered in seagull **splattts.** 'Blinking flying rats. They dive bomb us and pinch our food, keep us awake at night, dump on me nice clean car, harass the old folks, and they're so nosey, they're in the bins and bin bags, looking down people's chimneys and in through their windows…'

Nosey! Flying rats!! I was so angry that I chucked the magic chocolate bar on the floor.

Magically, the programme changed again!

I couldn't believe my luck. Result!! It was the cookery channel, and my favourite programme SupaChef, starring my own, the princess' *and* Mrs Baker's best of all time ever, ever favourite celebrity chef in the whole world…the lovely Mr Crispen Crackling.

Mr Crispen Crackling SupaChef

Today I had Mr Crispen Crackling to myself. No princess pestering and pecking me to go get her a take-away, no squabs squeaking and squealing and squabbling, no Mrs Baker passing me cakes and grub that I've got to eat right away (because I'm just a gull who can't say no!) and make me miss good bits of the programme. No, not today.

Today I could relax and enjoy the gullivision.

Mr Crispen Crackling, SupaChef, looked as gorgeous as usual. He had a long, lush and lovely, twisty, twiddly and twirly moustache, a proper moustache like all proper chefs should have, not a flea-bitten excuse for a toilet brush like some silly chefs sport.

He had two eyebrows. They were nice and bushy. One was always up, and one was always down, and it made him look inquisitive. That's like nosey, only more polite.

And he was polite as well.

His hair was nice and wavy and crinkly, like a crinkle cut oven chip, and some people say that Mr Crispen Crackling invented the crinkle cut oven chip because he's so clever. There is little doubt that he invented the potato crisp when he was just a baby, because he was a very clever baby, and that's why his mum and dad called him Crispen, and as for crackling (always the best bit of roast pork), well I believe him when he says he invented that too, because he's the best.

So be in no doubt that Mr Crispen Crackling, SupaChef, was the king of all celebrity chefs. Mrs Baker loved him, the princess worshipped him, and I, well I simply thought that the sun shone out of his artichokes.

'Well, my darlings,' he said. 'To finish the show today, or 'aujourd hui' as they say in France…'

He spoke lovely French, and twiddled his moustache as he did so. Nice.

'…I'm going to tell you about my new venture. Tomorrow I'm going to open my new restaurant, or as they say in France 'mon restaurant nouveau', down in Cornwall. It is going to be called Crackling's Crabery, and I hope you'll all come and visit me there for some real Cornish food, so until then goodbye or as they say 'en France – au revoir'…'

On the gullivision came a picture of a scrummy looking pasty. I couldn't help it. I'm not stupid and I knew it was only on the screen, but in a frenzy I tried to grab it, didn't I?

Well, I'm a gull right?
You know that.

What a swizz!

I was so excited that by accident I pecked one of the buttons on the front of the gullivision and Mr Crispen Crackling fizzled out as quickly as he had come on.

I stared at the screen. I couldn't see him or his nice hair, or his lovely, lovely moustache and inquisitive eyebrows. I couldn't hear him being polite or clever, or speaking bits of French. I certainly couldn't taste the pasty that had been on the screen, and what a blinking swizz that was.

I'd been watching the gullivision for a dangerously long time though, and was a bit worried about catching the screen scurvy or tellysquint or something worse. I hopped down and grabbed the magic chocolate bar for the princess; maybe she'd be able to break a bit off to eat, who knows?

Whatever, I had to tell her the exciting news about Mr Crispen Crackling, SupaChef, and his new Cornish celebrity restaurant.

I scuttled across the floor, up onto the soft chair, out through the window and onto the windowsill outside. I checked up, then down, the street. I hopped down, and then flapped up into the gullery to where the princess was sitting.

She didn't seem too interested in the magic bar of chocolate, but then she can be a funny gull at times. When I suggested she drop it to try and break off a chunk, she said that they weren't chunks. She said they were the buttons that Mrs Baker pressed to change the picture on the gullivision. She watched her do it all the time.

Right. A remote control. Silly me.

Anyway, the princess was excited about Mr Crispen Crackling coming to Cornwall and opening his restaurant, and she said that it would be nice for the gulls to have some decent gourmet food to pinch for a change.

I wonder exactly where he'll open it. It couldn't possibly be in *my* village, now could it?

That night, up in the gullery, as the princess and I roosted on our oh so comfortable featherbed of sharp sticks and brittle twigs and bits of orange coloured rope, amidst the faded empty bags of cheese and onion crisps and the fish skeletons, drying stinking strands of seaweed and half eaten nasty old pasties, I looked to the heavens above, to the stars.

To a star. To the star of stars. To Mr Crispen Crackling.

I drifted off into a deep, deep slumber, and I dreamed a dream.

The star of stars

I dreamt that it was the opening night of my new restaurant, Gully's Grubery, and there I was with all the press and TV people, and all the people of the village were there, and all my gull mates, and there were flags and stuff.

On the menu were all my favourite Cornish recipes and ingredients, all served in bin liners so the people could rip them open and get their heads right in and chuck the grub all over the shop in the proper manner.

And amongst the mix of nuggets and chips and nasty pasties, the dog fish tails and the starry gazy pie, between the crumbled, mouldy slices of saffron cake and Cornish cream teas and melted ice cream and stinking shellfish and rotting vegetables, nestled amidst the soggy battered sausages and mushed-up mushy peas and mashed up, messed up mashed potato and mackerel heads and yoghurts, there were greasy fish and chip wrappers and polystyrene cups and trays, cling film and bottles and empty bean cans smeared in their fluorescent orange sauce.

Yummy, yummy!

The dream feast went on long into the night, until the SupaChef himself, Mr Crispen Crackling, pulled his head from his bin liner and announced to all present that Gully's Grubery was in his humble opinion the top restaurant in the country and that I, Monsieur Gully, was top celebrity chef.

I stood tall on the table next to him and with my wing, I shook his hand.

Gully – Celebrity Chef.

I had finally arrived.

It was then that I was awoken by a loud cufuffle.

I had finally arrived

'Mind that wall! You don't want to knock her plant pots over!'

'All right, all right! Why do they build these stupid streets so narrow anyway?'

'That's it, that's right. Now come forward a bit…whoa!!'

There was the crash of a pot smashing. I peered over the edge of the gullery. Mrs Baker came to her door. In front of her lay her potted geranium, smashed on the road, and in front of that was a huge lorry with a satellite dish on the roof, and 'Star TV' painted on the side.

The driver got out, and came over to Mrs Baker.

'It's all right love,' he said. 'We're filming. We're a TV company.'

'But my pots…' she said.

'Don't worry love. Like I said, it's all right, we're from the telly,' he said, kicking the shards of pot away from the tyre. 'Close thing though, could have punctured my tyre. Still, no harm done.'

'But what about my potted flowers, dear?' she said.

He bent down and picked up the geranium, and threw it over a wall.

'That's better, now don't you worry about nothing, love. Like I said, we're from the telly. You know, cameras and that.'

'It's all very well,' said Mrs Baker. 'I've already had a treacle tart pinched this week.'

How utterly disgaceful! Who would do such a thing!?

'Come on George,' shouted the other from the cab, 'Give her a quid for the pot and let's get on. We got telly stuff and cameras and microphones and all that to do, it's TV init'!'

16

'Look love. I can't stop. Here's 20p for your pot, right. We're going down to film the opening of Mr Crispen Crackling's new restaurant for the telly, cos we're from the TV right? If you come on down, he might give you a sandwich or somefink darling. Did I mention that we're from the telly?'

'George!' shouted the other. 'Did you tell her we're from the telly?'

Although I was just beginning to get just a little bit cross about the pot, the man from the lorry had spoken the three magic words.

Mr Crispen Crackling.

It was an old pot anyway, and besides which the flowers were past their best, and I'm sure Mrs Baker didn't mind now that she knew the truth. Crackling's Crabery was to be in our village.

My village!

It was to be a grand affair, and the preparations continued most of the day. All the tables and chairs were brought outside the new restaurant by the harbour, and covered in crisp, white linen tablecloths. The whole area was festooned with bunting and nautical flags, and the restaurant sign was screwed up above the doorway.

Mr Crispen Crackling himself was busy writing the menu for the opening evening, sitting outside at one of his tables.

I had been watching from a nearby roof, and couldn't resist popping down to take a look.

After all, it's always nice to know what one might be having for supper.

I looked inquisitively over his shoulder and tried to read it. Oh my word, he was a clever one. Bits of it were written in French, like what he speaks. Then lots more of it read like a really good book with all big words and stuff. I cocked my head to one side, then the other, in an attempt to make sense of it.

I looked inquisitively over his shoulder

I was just wondering if potatoes got very hot in their jackets in the summertime, and whether you would eat crevettes or medallions of monkfish or wear them around your neck, when he turned and looked right at me.

His crinkly hair and magnificent moustache looked just like they did on the telly.

'Get lost. Go on, buzz off,' he said.

I could hardly believe it. The great Crispen Crackling SupaChef had spoken to me. Me! Just an ordinary gull. I was dumbstruck. He had taken time away from his busy schedule, on this of all days, to speak to me.

Oh all right. I know he told me to buzz off and get lost, but it was a start.

I could see that we were going to be great friends.

So I got the guys and gulls together and we began to make our own preparations for the opening, all in a row up on his roof, to make it an even more special day for him.

The seagull welcoming committee would give him a day that he would never forget.

Below, the TV men and their director were looking through their camera at the restaurant. It panned up to the roof. I struck my best pose; beak upwards, one eyebrow raised inquisitively like Crispen's, rakish smile, 'G' ring on my leg to camera. That sort of thing.

'Look at 'em up there,' said the cameraman. 'It's unnerving. What are they up to?'

'Crispen,' called the director to the SupaChef. 'Can we lose the gulls? They're going to spoil the shot.'

Crispen shrugged his shoulders.

'I don't think there's much we can do about them, my darling,' he said.

What are they up to?

'Well, I suppose they'll add a little local colour,' said the director, still looking up. 'But I don't like the look of that one with the ring on his leg much.'

The opening evening was spectacular. All the people of the village were there to see Mr Crispen Crackling cooking a huge cauldron of Cornish fish soup outside the restaurant, while the TV crew filmed the event. There was Mrs Baker, Boris, all the fishermen and artists, the shopkeepers and the man from the council and his sidekick Jasper, and Lionel and Honeysuckle and Tyrone had come down especially for the day, and there were curious visitors from all over, all wanting to see Mr Crispen Crackling SupaChef, the great man himself.

This, my darlings is a gurnard

With the camera taking a close-up, Crispen added a fish to the boiling, swirling, bubbling brew that passed as fish stew, first holding it up for the audience to see.

'Now this, my darlings, is a gurnard, and we're going to take the head and tail off, and then flake it into the fish stew, or as they say in France, the 'bouillabaise,' he said.

Well, I'm sorry, but I'm afraid that I misheard him.

I thought he said 'This here gurnard is especially for my new friend Gully.'

I dived down from the rooftop of the Crackling Crabery and snatched up the gurnard and whoomphed it down in one gulp as I flew up and away.

Crispen looked a little cross.

Well he can't have been cross with me, because we were going to be great mates.

He pointed his filleting knife up at me and scowled.

'Crispen,' snapped the director. 'The cameras, luvvie!'

'Sorry my darlings,' he said, forcing a smile. 'The gulls here are really cheeky, aren't they?'

'They're flying rats, my old son,' Lionel chipped in. 'You want to put a few of them in your stew thing!'

'Do you mean into 'le bouillabaisse', my darling?' asked Crispen, eyebrow raised to camera and moustache twitching.

'Yea, I'll catch 'em for you,' shouted Tyrone.

'So, my darlings if you'd like to take your seats, or 'asseyez vous' as they say in France, we can open the Crackling Crabery without further ado!'

As they took their places, I let out a loud squawking screech that echoed around the cliffs and harbourside.
Operation gourmet had been unleashed, and there was no looking back.

Crispen circulated amongst the tables, followed by the TV crew, and chatted to his guests. He stopped at Lionel's table.
'So, my darling, are you enjoying the special opening night fish stew?' he asked.
'Here Crisp, it's marvellous mind, and I'm a bit of a conny-sewer like, can't you tell?' asked Lionel. 'How much am I paying for this stewy stuff then?'
'It's £20 for 'le bouillabaise', my darling.'
'Crisp, that ain't enough. I'm going to give you thirty, right? Cos I got loads, mind,' said Lionel, his XXXXL T-shirt already heavily soiled with stew dribblings.
'That's very kind, my darling. Is that a tip?' said Crispen.
'No Crisp. If you wants a tip, I suggest you gets rid of all them stupid gulls on yer roof. Get yourself an airgun or summat.'
Crispen turned to the camera and smiled.
'Oh we couldn't possibly do that, could we my darlings? Mais non! They're part of the scene, the gulls. What would the place be without them?' he said, forcing another smile.
And of course he was right. What would the place be like? I could see that

Mr Crispen Crackling and I were indeed going to be great mates.

It was only right we should show our appreciation.

A special presentation of Cornish fayre was in order, I felt.

The first wave flew in from the west, in a classic V formation, armed with a deadly variety of Cornish ingredients, designed to inflict maximum Cornish flavours into the cauldron of fish stew.

The only slight flaw in the welcoming committee's plan was that seagulls have not as yet been equipped with laser guided technology, and that sadly there would be some collateral flavouring too.

The classic formation

In other words, it was likely that all the food would not end up in the pot!

They peeled off from their formation, and split into two separate strike units. One came in low from behind, up and over the roof of Crackling's Crabery, so low that I had to duck as they screeched overhead, and from the opposite direction came the others, high over the fish cellars and then diving down out of the sun's rays.

At first, the people didn't seem to realise what was happening. A bright yellow and mouldy slice of saffron cake came hurtling down and struck the restaurant sign, crumbling and showering those nearby in cake and currants, raisins and sultanas.

Honeysuckle laughed nervously.

She was first struck on the head by a jam covered scone, which fragmented and splashed into Lionel's fish soup, and then straight away she was struck again by a mackerel skeleton that draped itself across her head and hung down over her face.

Food began to fall all around as Operation gourmet got into full swing.

A Cornish ice cream plummeted down and stuck splosh on a man's head like a pointy clown's hat, a piece of heavy cake hit a plate and smashed it into pieces, a packet of ginger fairing biscuits landed and bobbed around in the fish stew, and blobs of clotted cream splattered everywhere like huge, heavy snow flakes.

Then came the wave of nasty pasties.

On impact, some shattered and exploded, showering the restaurant

customers in sliced potato and onion and chunks of well-seasoned skirt beef, and puffy, floury clouds of short crust pastry rose up and drifted across the tabletops like smoke across a battlefield.

There was widespread panic. The customers and staff and TV crew, covered now in a variety of Cornish ingredients, some savoury and others sweet, and wandering lost and confused in the explosion of the nasty pasty pastry mist, dived for cover into the fish cellars, the restaurant or under the tables, anywhere to escape the terrible, vicious yet nutritious, delicious deluge.

Only Lionel's table remained. He was so greedy that he was quite oblivious to the mayhem all around. A nasty pasty landed whole in his dish and splashed him with stew. He didn't even look up.

'Here my love,' he said to Honeysuckle, who was apparently in shock with the mackerel head still draped over her face and strawberry jam matted in her hair, 'This stew is marvellous mind. Mine come garnished with a scone and a whole pasty! Who'd have thought of doing that? He's a clever chef that Crisp!'

Mr Crispen Crackling, SupaChef, slumped open mouthed at his table, just outside the restaurant door.

He looked up at the skies.

He was so pleased that he could not even put it into words. The opening had gone swimmingly. Everyone had got to sample local food, and even if they hadn't got to eat any, everybody was at least now wearing some!

The TV crew came in for a close up.

'So, Crispen, how's it gone today?' asked the director.

'Yes, good,' said Crispen, quietly, staring straight ahead. 'Very good, my darlings. Or as they say in France, 'Tres bon.'

He looked up at me. I was pleased that we'd been able to help.

But he wasn't *looking* very pleased. I could tell by his eyebrows. Then, these TV chefs are all a tad temperamental. Perhaps he was a bit tired…

It was a few days later that I watched him come out of the door of Crackling's Crabery. He walked to the menu board and took out the old menu, and replaced it with a new one.

He looked up at me and I looked back.

His eyebrows still weren't right. They were both down and he looked like he was scowling. But it must have been a headache or maybe he had wind or something, because we're such good mates now, especially after that fabulous opening night extravaganza of grub.

When he'd gone in, I popped down to see the new menu, always an exciting moment.

It read 'Mouette rotie au vin rouge, served with local vegetables.'

It *sounded* delicious. Now unlike Mr Crispen Crackling, SupaChef, I don't speak much French, but that was roast something in red wine with local vegetables.

Fabulous. Anyone know what *mouette* is in English?

I can't wait to find out!

Also available

Three mischievous adventures of the wicked seagull on CD

  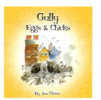

Visit the website to see the full range of Gully books and merchandise

www.thegullery.co.uk

Or phone The Gullery on 01208 880937

The Author

The creator, author and illustrator of Gully, Jon Cleave, lives in the heart of the lovely old Cornish fishing village of Port Isaac with his wife Caroline and boys Jakes, George and Theo.... oh yes, and hundreds and hundreds of squealing, squawking, screaming seagulls!